Lonely planet
Kids™

Amelia's MAZE ADVENTURE

Jane Gledhill

Hi, I'm **MARCO!**

And I'm **AMELIA!**

Help us travel a world
of mazes on a special mission,
and discover amazing facts along the way.
Are you up for the challenge? Then let's go!

AT LONELY PLANET HQ

Amelia and Marco have been called into HQ to help solve this international mystery. But they'll need your help!

LONELY PLANET BOSS
Amelia, head to the airport and get on the next flight to Paris. We need you to find those jewels before someone else does! Marco, stay at HQ with Lady Vivian and help Amelia retrace her steps. Use your phone to keep in touch.

MARCO
Got it, boss!

AMELIA
Don't worry, Lady Vivian. You can count on us! We'll have those jewels back in no time.

LADY VIVIAN
Oh, thank you, Amelia!

DUTY-FREE DASH

FLUMMOX RATING
3
Stuck? Solution on Page 88

END HERE!

PASSPORT

TAXI TO THE TOWER!

START HERE!

Help Amelia's taxi driver find his way through the busy Paris streets to meet Aurélie at the Eiffel Tower.

AMELIA: *Bonjour* Marco! I just landed in Paris.

MARCO: *Bonjour!* Did you find anything in the shop?

AMELIA: Yes, I found a bracelet! Here's a picture of it.

MARCO: Nice one! Now jump in a taxi to the Eiffel Tower. Lady Vivian's friend Aurélie Pinchart will meet you there. And guess what? You're going abseiling!

FLUMMOX RATING

2

Stuck? Solution on Page 88

HIDDEN GEM
Paris has been the capital of France since the year 508, and is one of the most-visited cities in the world.

END HERE!

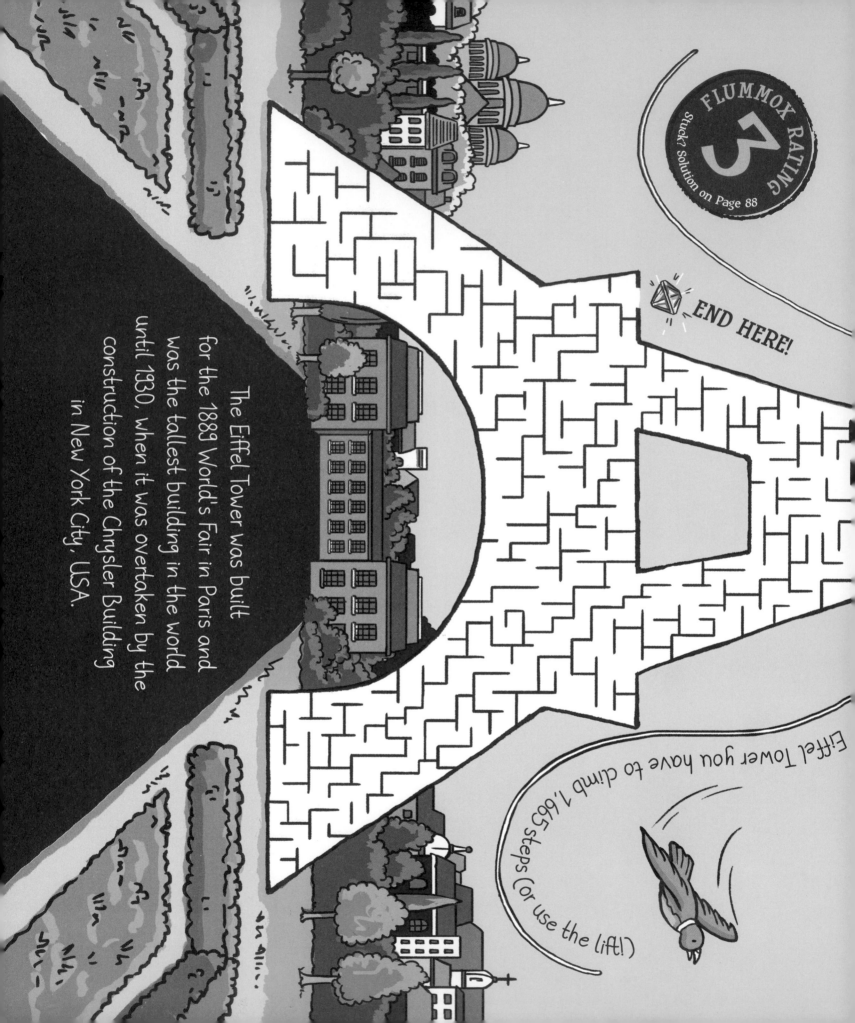

END HERE!

Eiffel Tower you have to climb 1,665 steps (or use the lift!)

The Eiffel Tower was built for the 1889 World's Fair in Paris and was the tallest building in the world until 1930, when it was overtaken by the construction of the Chrysler Building in New York City, USA.

MASKED BALL

Dance your way through the ballroom to find Lady Vivian's friend, Serena Gibbon.

START HERE!

LADY VIVIAN: Well done, Amelia! Now, can you find my friend Serena at the Palace of Versailles? She is attending a ball there and will take you on to Barcelona.

AMELIA: I've just arrived. Wow! This place is beautiful. I've never seen so much gold before!

The palace was built during the reign of King Louis XIV. It took over 30,000 workers to build it. Whole forests and swamps were moved to make way for its huge gardens!

HIDDEN GEM King Louis XIV loved shiny things so much that he had his palace covered with gold leaf and ate his dinner off solid gold plates. And if that wasn't enough bling, he could have a dance in his 75-metre-long mirrored ballroom after dinner.

END HERE!

FLUMMOX RATING
2
Stuck? Solution on Page 88

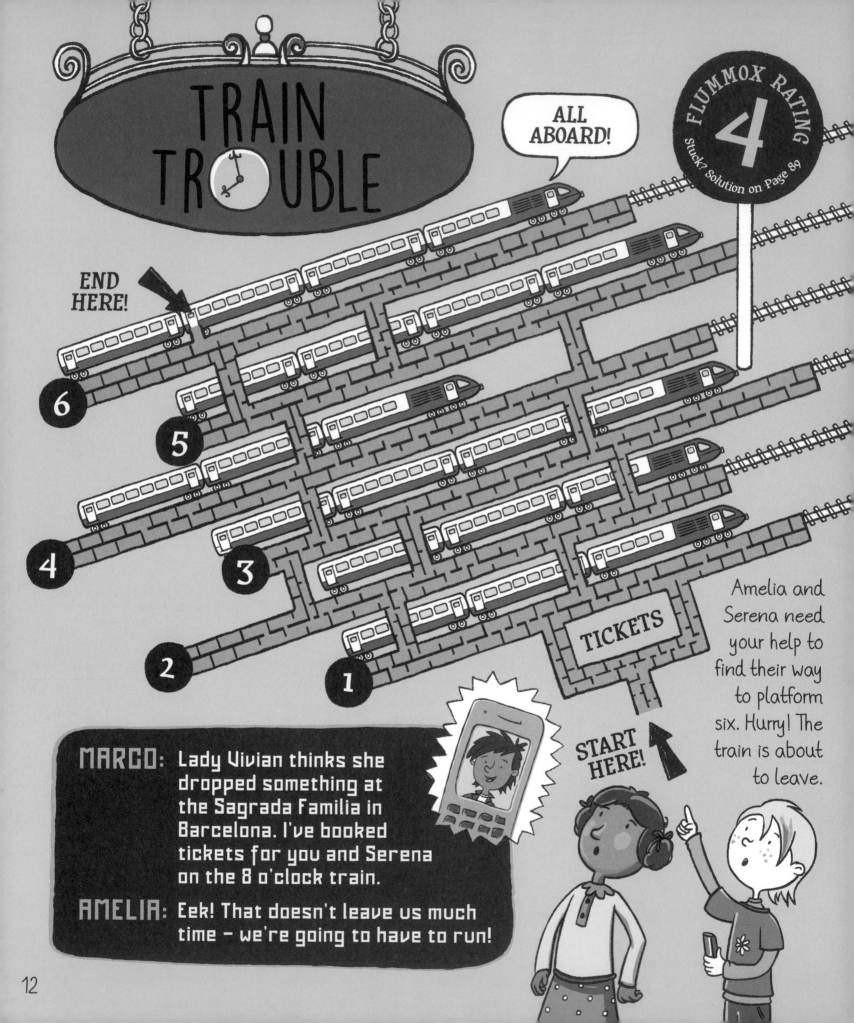

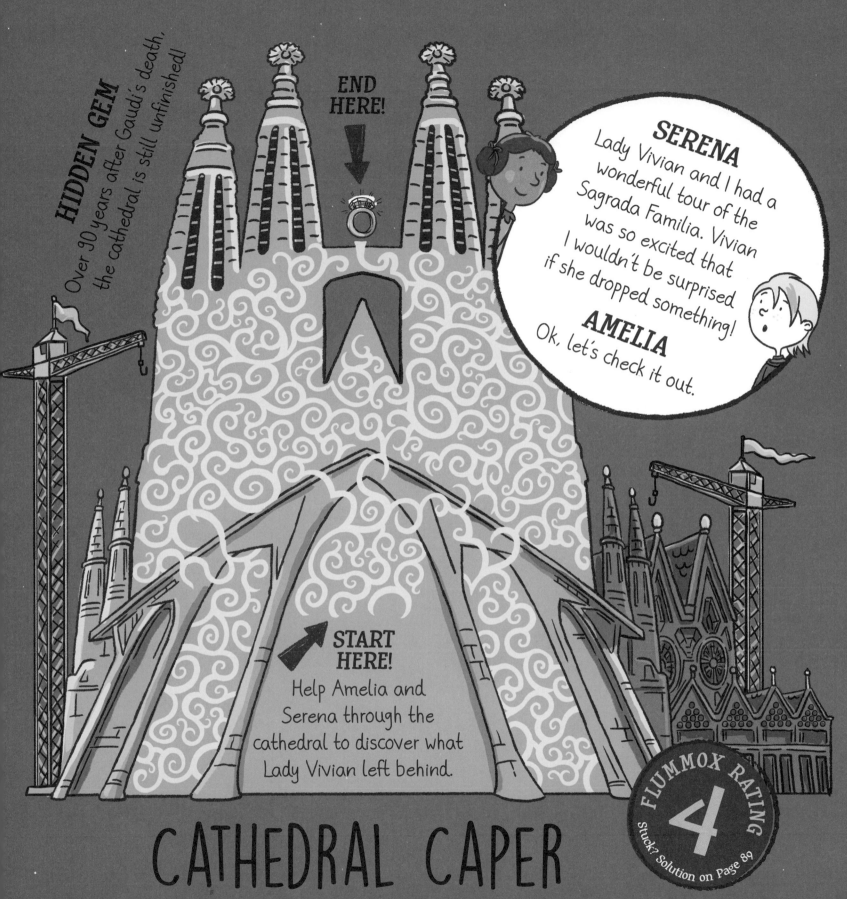

CATHEDRAL CAPER

The Sagrada Familia was designed by Antoni Gaudi. He created buildings with lots of curved lines because he believed there were no straight lines in nature.

END HERE!

FLUMMOX RATING
2
Stuck? Solution on Page 89

HIDDEN GEM
After the festival, the saucy streets of Buñol are washed clean with fire hoses.

15

FERRY ROUGH SEAS

AMELIA: Got the ticket, but I'm still trying to get the tomato seeds out of my hair! That was so much fun! Where now?

MARCO: The souk in Marrakesh. Lady Vivian dropped an earring there when she bought a scarf. The stall owner, Abdul Toubkal, has it.

AMELIA: Nice one! I'll go and pick it up.

Help the ferry sail safely through the choppy waves to the port in Morocco.

START HERE!

Stuck? Solution on Page 89

SOUK SEEKER

A souk is a marketplace where you can buy pottery, textiles, spices and almost anything else you can think of. The stalls at a souk are usually very close together and it can be easy to get lost.

MARCO: Try not to get too distracted on your way to the Scarf Emporium! Remember you're on a mission, not a shopping trip!

AMELIA: Cheeky! If you're not careful, I won't bring you back a present!

Find your way through the basket weave to help Amelia pick up the earring from Abdul and continue her mission.

START HERE!

FLUMMOX RATING **3** Stuck? Solution on Page 89

END HERE!

HIDDEN GEM
You can get some great bargains in a souk because you are expected to haggle over the price of what you want to buy.

WAY OUT

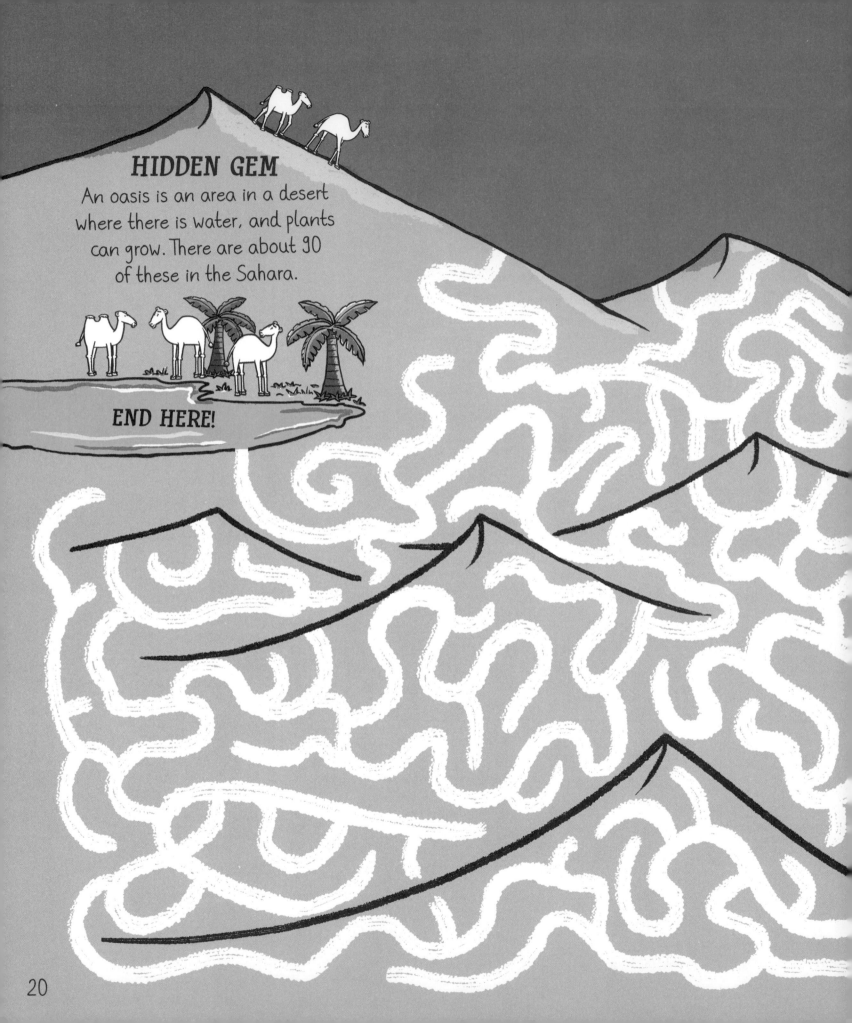

HIDDEN GEM

An oasis is an area in a desert where there is water, and plants can grow. There are about 90 of these in the Sahara.

END HERE!

Help Amelia and Hassan drive the dune buggy through the shifting sands of the Sahara to reach the oasis.

MARCO: Are those camels I can see? Where are you?

AMELIA: In the Sahara. We're trying to track down the camel Lady V went trekking on.

MARCO: Don't upset it – I've heard they spit! When you find it, head to Cairo to meet Dr Miriam Shortstaff at the Egyptian Museum.

START HERE!

Help Amelia through the confusion of camels to find what fell out of Lady Vivian's bag.

HIDDEN GEM Camels are called 'ships of the desert' because the rocking motion you feel when riding them can make you seasick.

END HERE!

FLUMMOX RATING
1
Stuck? Solution on Page 89

CROCODILE COMMOTION

The Temple of Kom Ombo was built to worship the Egyptian crocodile god Sobek. Many years ago, sacred crocodiles would lie in the sun around the temple.

END HERE!

FLUMMOX RATING

1

Stuck? Solution on Page 96

HIDDEN GEM

The Masai Mara National Reserve is named after the Maasai people who live there and the Mara River that winds its way through the park. It is home to lions, elephants, rhinoceros and many other wild animals.

END HERE!

FLUMMOX RATING

2

Stuck? Solution on Page 90

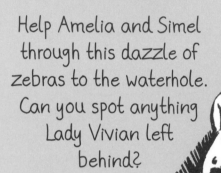

Help Amelia and Simel through this dazzle of zebras to the waterhole. Can you spot anything Lady Vivian left behind?

START HERE!

ZIGZAGGING THROUGH ZEBRAS!

END HERE!

HIDDEN GEM

Each year more than 1.5 million wildebeest and around 250,000 zebras make the long journey in search of food from the Serengeti National Park in Tanzania to the Masai Mara National Reserve in Kenya. It is one of the largest and most spectacular migrations on the planet.

STORMY SKY SLALOM

AMELIA: Bingo, I found a bangle!

MARCO: Great job! There's a plane waiting at the campsite to take you to the Maldives. I hope you packed your snorkel!

AMELIA: I did! Can't wait for a swim – it's boiling hot here on safari.

Guide Amelia's plane through the storm clouds to clearer skies.

START HERE!

END HERE!

FLUMMOX RATING
3
Stuck? Solution on Page 90

HIDDEN GEM
The Maldives, in the Indian Ocean, is made up of over 1,200 coral islands, none of which rise higher than 1.8 metres above sea level.

SNORKEL SCRAMBLE

START HERE!

Help Amelia find her mask, fins and snorkel
and make it to the kayak to go snorkelling.

FLUMMOX RATING
3
Stuck? Solution on Page 91

FLUMMOX RATING

2

Stuck? Solution on Page 91

END HERE!

HIDDEN GEM

The Indian Ocean around the Maldives is home
to five of the seven different species of sea turtle
in the world, including the green turtle and
the hawksbill turtle.

END HERE!

JELLYFISH JUMBLE

HIDDEN GEM

A jellyfish's tentacles are covered with stinging cells that are sensitive to touch. When one of these cells is triggered, it sends out a harpoon-like spike filled with venom that can stick to your skin and give you a nasty sting.

TAJ MAZE—HAL

The Taj Mahal in Agra, India, is one of the most beautiful buildings in the world. Emperor Shah Jahan built it as a memorial to his third wife, Mumtaz Mahal, who died in childbirth.

HIDDEN GEM

The emperor who built the Taj Mahal was so broken-hearted by the loss of his wife that it is said his hair turned grey overnight.

END HERE!

TIARAS AT TEA TIME

AMELIA: Hi Marco! We're finally here in Darjeeling. I'm looking forward to a nice cup of tea.

MARCO: Don't sit around chatting over a cuppa for too long! I need you to head to Everest to meet Sherpa Gyalzen as soon as you're done.

END HERE!

FLUMMOX RATING
3
Stuck? Solution on Page 91

HIDDEN GEM
The name Darjeeling comes from the Tibetan words 'dorje' (thunderbolt) and 'ling' (place).

The town of Darjeeling in West Bengal, India, is famous all over the world for its lush tea plantations that grow delicious black tea.

Help Amelia and Verity weave their way through the tea plantation to discover what Lady V left behind.

START HERE!

43

SUMMIT SPARKLING

Mount Everest in the Himalayas stands at 8,848 metres tall and is the highest mountain in the world.

AMELIA
Wow, what an incredible view! Lady Vivian said that you took her on an expedition up the mountain. Do you think she might have dropped anything on the way?

GYALZEN
Let's retrace our steps. You never know!

Help Amelia and Sherpa Gyalzen get to the summit and find the jewel. Then can you help them to find their way back down again?

START HERE!

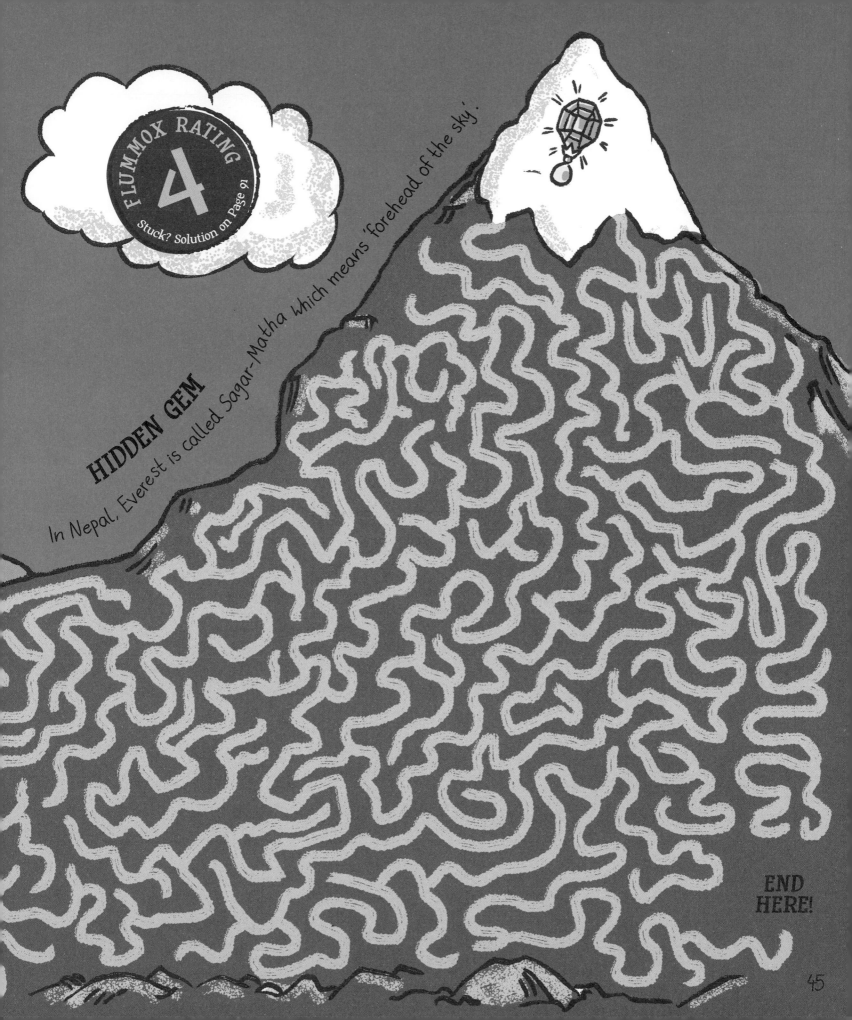

Stuck? Solution on Page 91

NOM NOM NOODLES

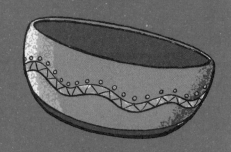

AMELIA: That climb was amazing, but my feet hurt. Any chance of a rest?

MARCO: No time! Next up, Beijing. Meet Lady V's friend Amy at the noodle factory. She'll take you to see Li Li Huang, a Great Wall of China guide.

FLUMMOX RATING

3

Stuck? Solution on Page 92

START HERE!

Guide Amelia through the knot of noodles to find Amy.

Beijing is the capital of the People's Republic of China. Beijing has been an important city in China for over 3,000 years. It has had many names including Peking, Jingcheng and Yangjing.

END HERE!

HIDDEN GEM
Be careful not to break the noodles. In China, noodles are a symbol of long life and it is considered bad luck to cut them into shorter pieces.

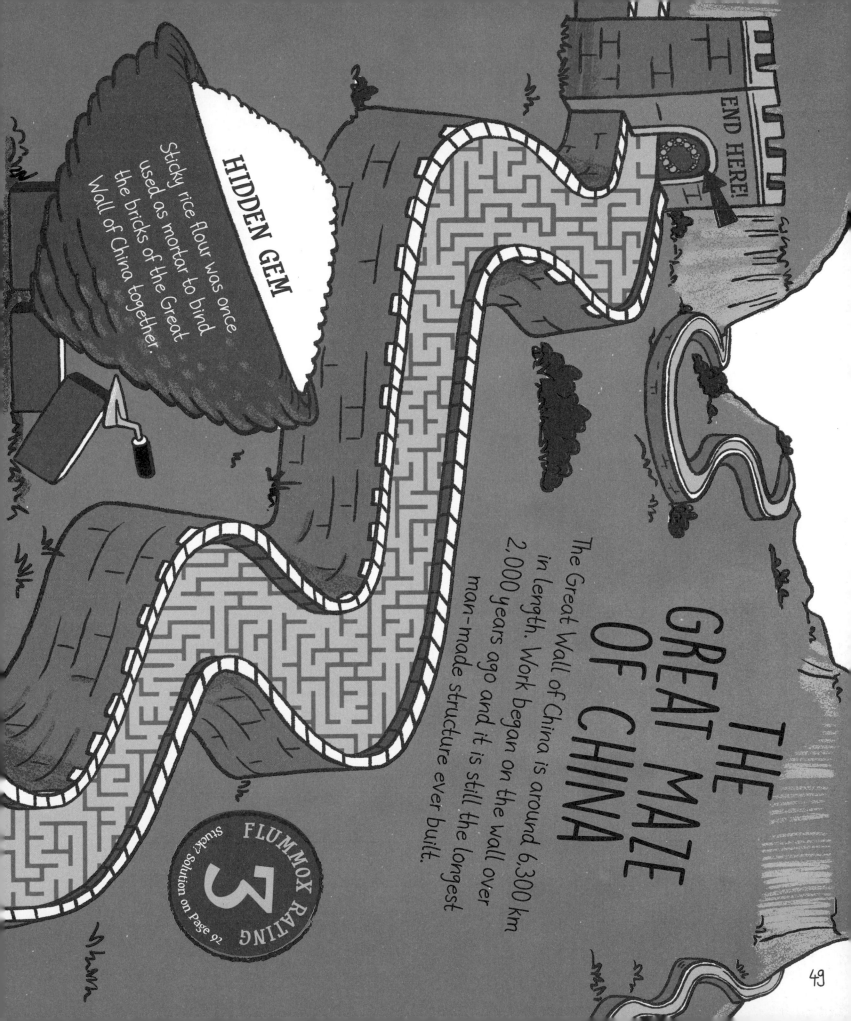

THE GREAT MAZE OF CHINA

The Great Wall of China is around 6,300 km in length. Work began on the wall over 2,000 years ago and it is still the longest man-made structure ever built.

HIDDEN GEM

Sticky rice flour was once used as mortar to bind the bricks of the Great Wall of China together.

FLUMMOX RATING

3

Stuck? Solution on Page 92

END HERE!

KAWAII CRAZY

AMELIA: Let Lady Vivian know we found her bracelet!

MARCO: Great work in China! Now for something completely different! Head to Tokyo, Japan, to meet Ria Taki at the kawaii convention. She will take you on to the city of Kyoto.

AMELIA: Kawaii? Cute! On my way.

Help Amelia find her way through the convention to find Ria Taki.

START HERE!

Tokyo is the capital of Japan. It is home to over 33 million people, making it the largest city in the world. Even though Tokyo is a very busy and important city, the Japanese love of all things kawaii or 'cute' is everywhere.

END HERE!

FLUMMOX RATING
1
Stuck? Solution on Page 92

HIDDEN GEM
Kawaii isn't just for kids. From bus stops shaped like giant fruit to frog-shaped construction signs - Kawaii is everywhere and for everyone.

51

KYOTO GO!

FLUMMOX RATING 4 Stuck? Solution on Page 92

END HERE!

The city of Kyoto used to be the capital of Japan. In fact, the word 'kyoto' means 'capital' in Japanese. Kyoto is considered to be one of the world's most beautiful cities, famous for its temples, festivals and incredible cherry blossom in spring.

START HERE!

RIA
Lady Vivian and I hosted a charity tea ceremony in a garden in Kyoto. Maybe she left something behind.

AMELIA
Sounds promising. Let's check it out.

Guide Amelia and Ria through the ripples in this koi pond to find what Lady Vivian left behind.

HIDDEN GEM
Some koi carp live for over 200 years and are incredibly valuable. Certain very special fish have sold for well over a million pounds.

MARCO: What did you find?

AMELIA: A ring! The garden was beautiful.

MARCO: Nice! Make your way to Bangkok now. You need to meet Dang Aromdee at his Caving Supply Shop to get kitted out for your next expedition – underground!

Bangkok is the bustling capital of Thailand. It is hot and has lots of traffic, but is filled with friendly people and the smell of delicious food.

START HERE!

Help Amelia through the tangled tuk-tuk traffic to find Dang Aromdee's Caving Supply Shop.

HIDDEN GEM
Tuk-tuks are three-wheeled motorised taxis found all over Thailand. They get the name 'tuk-tuk' from the sound made by their engines.

TUK >

< TUK

TRAFFIC >

FLUMMOX RATING
3
Stuck? Solution on Page 92

CAVING
SUPPLY
SHOP

← END HERE

WHAT'S IN THE WATERFALL?

AMELIA
Hi Dang! Lady Vivian said you took her caving in Doi Phuka National Park. She dropped her backpack into a waterfall. Do you think something could have fallen out?

DANG
Let's go and see. Mind your head!

Help Dang and Amelia through the cave systems to find the waterfall and discover what fell out of Lady Vivian's backpack.

START HERE!

FLUMMOX RATING 2
Stuck? Solution on Page 93

HIDDEN GEM

Animals that have evolved to live their whole lives in caves are called troglobites. Many troglobites are blind, but they are all perfectly adapted to the dark, difficult conditions.

END HERE!

57

BORDER BOTHER

AMELIA: Phew, it's good to be above ground again. And we found a necklace!

MARCO: Great job! Now you need to make your way to Angkor in Cambodia. It's temple time!

START HERE!

Help Amelia and Dang drive his pick-up truck across the Thai border into Cambodia. Watch out for potholes!

HIDDEN GEM

No one is quite sure why the city of Angkor was abandoned. Perhaps people left the city due to a series of floods or fled because of an outbreak of a disease.

FLUMMOX RATING
3
Stuck? Solution on Page 93

The city of Angkor was once one of the largest cities in the world. It is now famous for its long-abandoned temples, some of which are over a thousand years old.

BORDER CONTROL

END HERE!

MARCO: I've just had a look at Lady Vivian's photos. There's one of her at the Bayon Temple with something shiny hanging out of her bag. Can you take a look?

AMELIA: We're on our way!

FLUMMOX RATING 4 Stuck? Solution on Page 93

At the top of each of Bayon's towers there are four faces, each looking in a different direction. The faces are said to be of the Buddhist god Lokeshvara, who sent out kindness in four directions.

Can you help Amelia and Dang through the temple to find what fell from Lady Vivian's bag?

START HERE!

TROUBLE AT THE TEMPLE

END HERE!

HIDDEN GEM

Some temples in the Angkor region have been left as they were discovered, with trees growing out of their roofs and doorways.

AMELIA: It was one of Lady Vivian's tiaras! What's next?

MARCO: Good find! I've sent you a link to an animal sanctuary in Borneo. They've reported an orangutan carrying a brooch. Can you check it out?

START HERE!

Guide Amelia up through the trees to find Lady Vivian's brooch. Watch out for giant snakes!

ORANGU-TANGLE

The jungles of Borneo are home to lots of different plants and animals, including orangutans. The word 'orangutan' means 'man of the forest' in the Malay language.

HIDDEN GEM

According to Borneo legend, the Nabau was a 30-metre-long, man-eating snake with the head of a dragon. Some people believe this serpent still lurks within the jungle.

END HERE!

FLUMMOX RATING

2

Stuck? Solution on Page 95

MAKING TRACKS OUTBACK

The Outback is the common name for the vast desert that makes up much of central Australia. It is home to venomous creatures such as snakes, spiders and scorpions as well as famous landmarks such as Uluru.

END HERE!

HIDDEN GEM
Uluru is 348 metres tall and was known as Ayers Rock before being given back to the local Aboriginal people.

GREAT BARRIER THIEF

The Great Barrier Reef is over 2,300 km long and is the largest reef system in the world. It is made up of over 2,500 individual reefs and is home to over 400 species of coral.

HIDDEN GEM
Sunscreen and oils in your skin are poisonous to the coral - they can stop it from growing and even kill it completely.

END HERE!

The Galapagos Islands lie about 1,000 km off the coast of Ecuador in South America. Their remote location makes them home to some amazing and unique animals, including the giant Galapagos tortoise.

AMELIA
What huge tortoises! Hello, you must be Professor Snapdragon. Can you help me find some lost jewels?

PROFESSOR SNAPDRAGON
Of course! I'll take you to Machu Picchu where Vivian and I met. But first, can you help me clean up this beach?

Help Amelia and Professor Snapdragon tiptoe around the tortoises as they collect litter.

START HERE!

TIPTOE THROUGH THE TORTOISES

FLUMMOX RATING 1
Stuck? Solution on Page 94

END HERE!

HIDDEN GEM
The word 'galápago' means turtle in Spanish. These giant tortoises are some of the longest-living creatures on Earth, some living for well over 100 years!

Machu Picchu is the remains of a stone citadel built by a great South American civilization called the Incas around the year 1450. It lies 2,400 metres above sea level in the Peruvian Andes mountains and is surrounded by lush jungle and mountain mists.

FLUMMOX RATING
5
Stuck? Solution on Page 94

HIDDEN GEM
The stones used to build Machu Picchu don't have anything sticking them together. The Inca builders shaped the stones to fit together almost perfectly.

END HERE!

The Amazon River is 6,400 km long and is the second-longest river in the world after the River Nile. It runs through the Amazon Rainforest and is home to many species of fish including meat-eating piranhas.

END HERE!

HIDDEN GEM
Although piranhas have a hefty bite, they are unlikely to attack you unless they are very hungry, or if you mess with their eggs.

FLUMMOX RATING
3
Stuck? Solution on Page 94

END HERE!

FLUMMOX RATING
3
Stuck? Solution on Page 94

HIDDEN GEM
Toucans use their large bills to help them reach fruit growing on branches that wouldn't be able to support their weight.

MEXICAN WAVE

HIDDEN GEM

Mexico City was built on the ruins of an Aztec city called Tenochtitlan. Unfortunately, Tenochtitlan was built on a lake, so now some parts of Mexico City are sinking!

END HERE!

FLUMMOX RATING
5
Stuck? Solution on Page 94

CHICHEN ITZA

END HERE!

El Castillo, or the Temple of Kukulkan, was built by an ancient civilization called the Maya over 1,000 years ago. As well as being a temple, the pyramid was also a Mayan calendar.

HIDDEN GEM
Twice each year – in spring and in autumn – the sun is in the correct position to cast the shadow of a snake slithering down the north side of the pyramid.

SHOE SHOPPING SPREE

One of the most famous cities in the world, New York is a popular shopping destination. It is made up of five boroughs: Manhattan, Brooklyn, the Bronx, Staten Island and Queens.

END HERE!

HIDDEN GEM

New York is sometimes called the Big Apple. It is said that this is because, when times were hard, people travelled into the city to sell apples on the street.

81

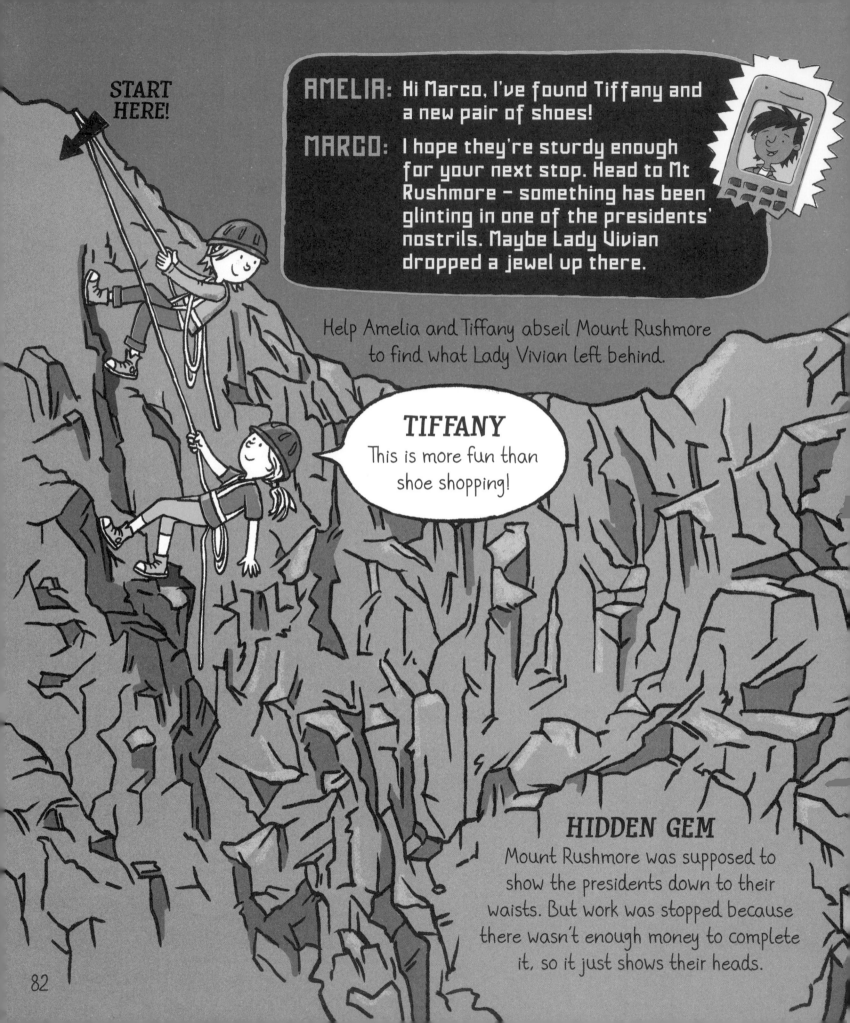

IN A RUSH—MORE!

Mount Rushmore National Memorial is a sculpture of the faces of former US presidents George Washington, Thomas Jefferson, Theodore Roosevelt and Abraham Lincoln. It is carved directly into the side of Mount Rushmore in South Dakota, USA.

FLUMMOX RATING
5
Stuck? Solution on Page 95

END HERE!

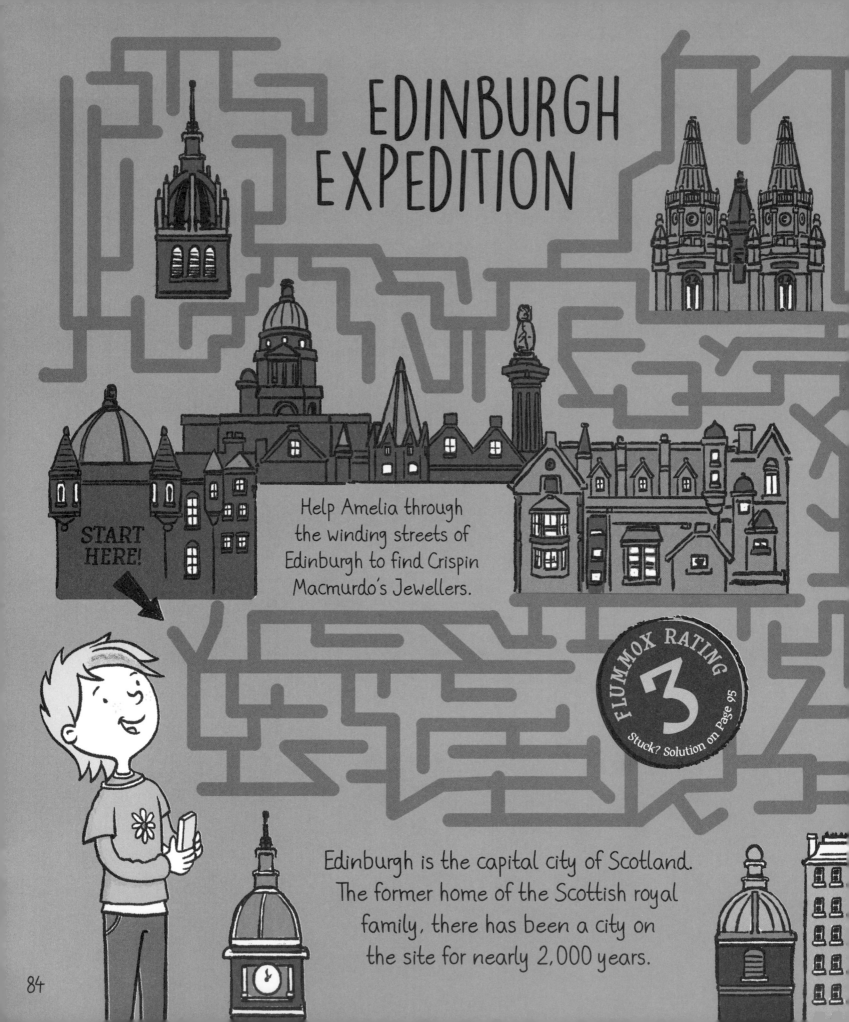

EDINBURGH EXPEDITION

START HERE!

Help Amelia through the winding streets of Edinburgh to find Crispin Macmurdo's Jewellers.

FLUMMOX RATING
3
Stuck? Solution on Page 95

Edinburgh is the capital city of Scotland. The former home of the Scottish royal family, there has been a city on the site for nearly 2,000 years.

GOING UNDERGROUND

AMELIA: Hi Marco! I've got all the jewels packed safely in the jewellery box and I'm back in London.

MARCO: Welcome home! Lady Vivian is here now, so why don't you hop on the tube and meet us at Lonely Planet HQ.

AMELIA: On my way. See you soon!

Help Amelia navigate the London Underground to reach Lonely Planet HQ on the South Bank.

START HERE!

HIDDEN GEM
In the Second World War, a section of the Central Line of the Underground was used as a factory for aircraft parts.

Amelia's MAZE SOLUTIONS
PAGES 4–23

PAGES 4–5: DUTY-FREE DASH

PAGES 6–7: TAXI TO THE TOWER!

PAGES 8–9: TOWER OF TRINKETS

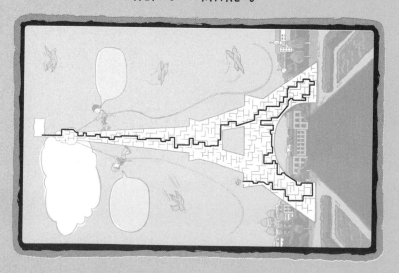

PAGES 10–11: MASKED BALL

PAGES 12–13: TRAIN TROUBLE/CATHEDRAL CAPER

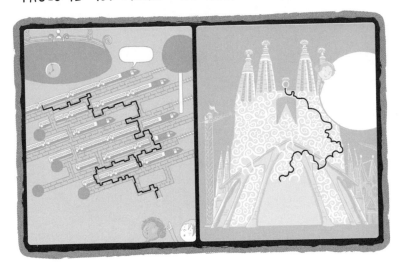

PAGES 14–15: TOMATINA TANGLE

PAGES 16–17: FERRY ROUGH SEAS

PAGES 18–19: SOUK SEEKER

PAGES 20–21: SAND DUNE SCRAMBLE

PAGES 22–23: CAMEL TRAIN CONFUSION

Amelia's MAZE SOLUTIONS
PAGES 24–45

PAGES 24–25: MAYHEM AT THE MUSEUM

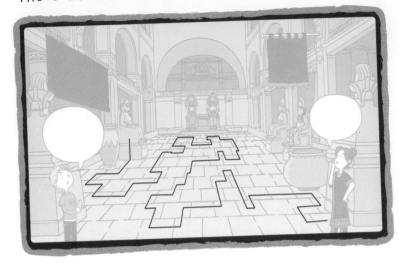

PAGES 26–27: CROCODILE COMMOTION

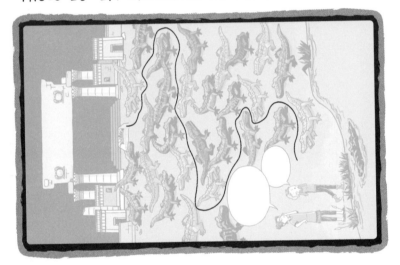

PAGES 28–29: JEEP SAFARI

PAGES 30–31: ZIGZAGGING THROUGH ZEBRAS

PAGES 32–33: STORMY SKY SLALOM

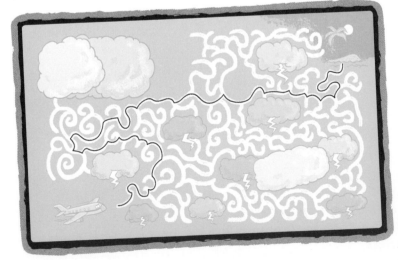

PAGES 34–35: SNORKEL SCRAMBLE

PAGES 36–37: KAYAK CAPER

PAGES 38–39: JELLYFISH JUMBLE

PAGES 40–41: TAJ MAZE-HAL

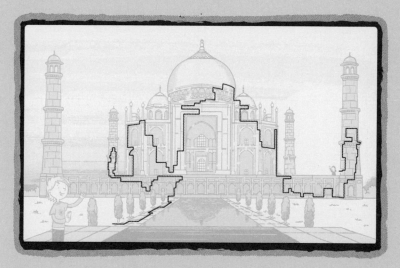

PAGES 42–43: TIARAS AT TEA TIME

PAGES 44–45: SUMMIT SPARKLING

Amelia's MAZE SOLUTIONS
PAGES 46–67

PAGES 46–47: NOM NOM NOODLES

PAGES 48–49: THE GREAT MAZE OF CHINA

PAGES 50–51: KAWAII CRAZY

PAGES 52–53: KYOTO GO

PAGES 54–55: TUK-TUK TRAFFIC

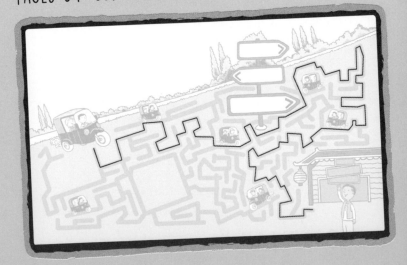

PAGES 56–57: WHAT'S IN THE WATERFALL?

PAGES 58–59: BORDER BOTHER

PAGES 60–61: TROUBLE AT THE TEMPLE

PAGES 62–63: ORANGU-TANGLE

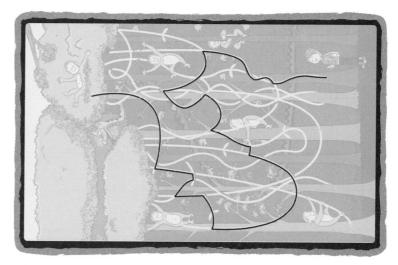

PAGES 64–65: MAKING TRACKS OUTBACK

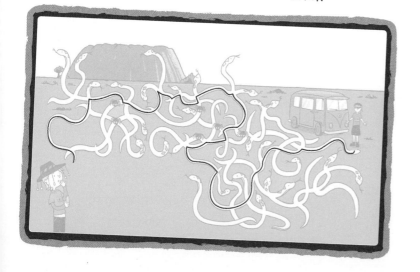

PAGES 66–67: GREAT BARRIER THIEF

Amelia's MAZE SOLUTIONS

PAGES 68–86

PAGES 68–69: TIPTOE THROUGH THE TORTOISES

PAGES 70–71: MUCH TO DO IN MACHU PICCHU

PAGES 72–73: A-MAZE-ON RIVER RAFTING

PAGES 74–75: SNEAKY BEAKY

PAGES 76–77: MEXICAN WAVE

PAGES 78–79: CHICHEN ITZA

PAGES 80–81: SHOE SHOPPING SPREE

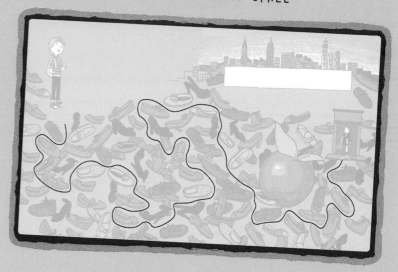

PAGES 82–83: IN A RUSH—MORE

PAGES 84–85: EDINBURGH EXPEDITION

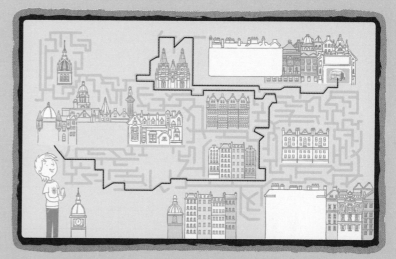

PAGES 86–87: GOING UNDERGROUND

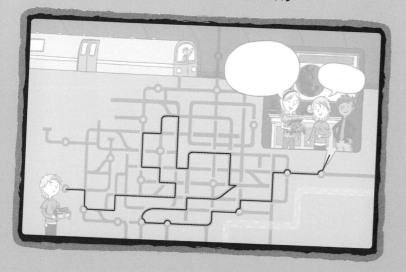

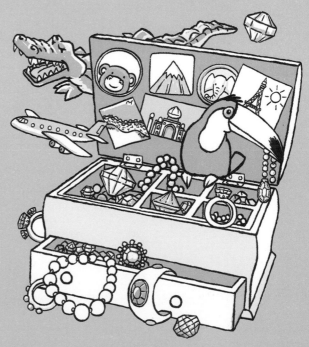

Amelia's MAZE ADVENTURE

Published in May 2017
by Lonely Planet Global Limited
CRN: 554153
ISBN: 978 1 78657 435 0
www.lonelyplanetkids.com
© Lonely Planet 2017

10 9 8 7 6 5 4 3 2 1

Printed in China

Commissioned and project managed by Dynamo Limited
Author: Jane Gledhill
Editor: Dynamo Limited
Design: Dynamo Limited
Illustration: Dynamo Limited
Publishing Director: Piers Pickard
Publisher: Tim Cook
Commissioning Editors: Jen Feroze and Catharine Robertson
Print production: Larissa Frost and Nigel Longuet

With thanks to: Christina Webb

LONELY PLANET OFFICES

STAY IN TOUCH
lonelyplanet.com/contact

AUSTRALIA
The Malt Store, Level 3, 551 Swanston St, Carlton, Victoria 3053
T: 03 8379 8000

IRELAND
Unit E, Digital Court, The Digital Hub,
Rainsford St, Dublin 8

USA
124 Linden St, Oakland, CA 94607
T: 510 250 6400

UK
240 Blackfriars Rd, London SE1 8NW
T: 020 3771 5100

MIX
Paper from
responsible sources
FSC
www.fsc.org   FSC™ C021741

Paper in this book is certified against the
Forest Stewardship Council™ standards.
FSC™ promotes environmentally responsible,
socially beneficial and economically viable
management of the world's forests.